A LIFE LESS

SPOKEN

CRYSTAL ELLISON

About the Author

Crystal Ellison was born and raised in Knoxville, TN. She eventually moved out west and now lives in New Mexico. The most important to Crystal in life is her children and family. Crystal has had a long time passion in writing poetry at a young age. She is a first time author. "A life less spoken" was inspired due to the tragic loss of her son. She expresses her emotions through her words. As she pours her heart and soul onto these pages she created, she wants to give people hope. Due to her situation involving her son's passing she not only wrote this book, she is trying to pass "The Isaiah Nordgren Law" Crystal is also trying to spread the word of Suicide Awareness as well.

"I want to go to college and take nursing So I can join the military and become a medic"
-Isaiah Nordgren

"I don't know why things happen the way they do, but we just gotta get through them"
-Caleb Nordgren

"Love is what holds people, Love is better when people are with their family that keep them away from hate, and found by hope. Family is the love, pure joy and happiness. From the good times to the bad, family won't let you down, where family come together for love and peace family will always be a part of me. During the times we are together seem that mean the most to me. During a time of grief, we stick together like glue. We may have disagreements, but we always come through. We are the family that stays by each other side and never goes away. We are family we are here to stay"
-Christian Nordgren

"It's okay not to be okay. It's okay to cry. It's okay to let all emotions out. Even if screaming helps, scream. Do what you need to do in that minute"
-Crystal Ellison

"When I lost my son, writing was really one of the very few ways to help me through my grieving. It's like God took my hands and I could not stop writing. Then I wrote so much I decided to make a book out of it. When my son passed I decided enough was enough and I would not be silent anymore. I need to help others who have been in my situation. My life has been a winding road for many miles, many of years. I put my screams and anger and emotions into these words. Hear me through this book.

I want to add mental illness is nothing to be ashamed or embarrassed of. If you have someone you know or yourself, please get help immediately. Everyone's life has a purpose.

I hope it helps you find some peace, understanding, hope, and faith. Most of all that you are not alone.

A Life Less Spoken is in the memory of my son Isaiah J. Nordgren. I have put a lot of emotions and soul into this book. This book is very personal to me. It means a lot and I am proud of this accomplishment".

Contents

A Part of an Angel's Wing

The moment you arrived, so much joy and love rushed through our
lives.
I never knew what unconditional love was until you were lying in my
arms with tears in my eyes.
praying for a miracle the day you arrived.
Now I look back, seeing you through God's eyes.
giving you to me and my family,
not knowing you only have a limited time to spend with us.
Your departure from this life has been devastating to us.

I only wish I knew what was weighing on your tender heart.
I would have helped take the pain away.
Now you are gone. You left this world without a word to say.
I only have what God gave me.
a part of an angel's wing;
Now you are in heaven, hearing the angels sing.

I do not know how life is going to be without you here.
There is so much to say and do.
I promise you now that I will never forget you, my son.
A part of an angel wing is all I have left.
I will never forget the sound of your voice.
or the twitch in your face when you laugh.
Or the tears you cried on my shoulder.
So many of us miss you dearly.
You will never be replaced.
I know I'm not the only one who has lost you.
You are the missing piece that will always be empty.

A part of an angel's wing is what I hold.
Now you are in God's hands.
Wings of white and streets of gold
It's time to take your wings and fly.
a part of an angel's wing that will be forever loved, but this is not a
goodbye.
I will treasure you, my son, and the time we had.
an angel's wing that I held in my hands and close to my heart.

We will all look up to the sky and hope to see a glimpse of part of an angel's wing as we watch you fly and sing.

Forever 21

Forever twenty-one, you are in our eyes.
Barely starting out to live your own life
So many dreams you had lay in your heart and mind.
So young to go
Too young to die
Life can be cruel sometimes.
I only wish I knew exactly what rest on your mind.
Forever twenty-one
I will never see you turn twenty-two.
The plans you made
The work you have done
A mother who will always be proud of her son
Forever twenty-one, I see a young man who left us too soon.
A mother I see, a son I have to live the rest of my life without you

<u>Drained</u>

Slow motion I feel when I move
Walking as if I have strings attached to my body
I have no clue where I am going.
I turned into a zombie.

I'm dead walking in my shoes.
Lord, why do I feel this way?
I hope I don't live like this another day.
Energy is what I need.
lack of strength in my soul
Inside, I bleed

Nothing else is left within me.
no sign of life,
Take what is left of me, Lord.
Emptiness is all I feel inside.

How do I deal with the pain?

As some ask me, "How do you deal with the pain?"
I simply reply, "I have no choice, but to live with the pain."
I feel as if I've gone insane.
This pain is like luggage I carry with me wherever I go.
No matter how far I travel, this pain will always go with me.

I dream you are still with me.
I dream you are alive, standing beside me.
I hear sympathy from so many
I do not want sympathy.
I just want my son.
I always told you I loved you to infinity and beyond.
Now this pain carries itself within me.
Deep down in my heart and soul
I know this new pain has scarred every inch of me.

too deep to cover up;
As days and nights come and go, this pain still remains in my soul.
I do not know the pain you were in.
I do feel pain, which I cannot explain.
As I travel this life, you will always be with me.
I would do anything if I could see you alive once again.

<u>Celebrate</u>

Celebrating my son's life
Only cry happy tears because you've flown up in the sky
Celebrating you who was in our lives, it is hard to hold the pain back.
We still cry.
Cherishing the time we had
Treasure the memories we have. Your life will not be forgotten.
The love we have for you will never die.
As we celebrate you down here on earth
Wishing you knew how much we love you still, we will all miss you as
the days go by. We celebrate you, son, as you fly up to the sky.

Broken hearted

Broken hearted I stand here today
Trying to pick up the pieces that got shattered away
Too many pieces I try to find
It seems I can't find every piece of this heart of mine

My heart seems to be out of rhythm, out of rhyme
Sometimes it is hard to breathe.
It hurts every time
One day I hope to gather all the pieces of my broken heart
Until then all I do is fall apart

Broken hearted I may be for a while
This road that I travel on is a winding and cold
I will never know how to find all the pieces on this difficult road
As I pray for a miracle during this time
All I will do is try to have the courage to fix this broken heart of mine

<u>Courage</u>

Jesus, give me the courage to live. Let me live, being brave to see a
new day.
Give me strength to move forward with this pain.
When I wake up in the morning, I turn to you. Only you can help me
through.

Photos

As I look at photos of you and our family, I miss these days when you
were here. I keep the photos of me and you so close and near.
Photos of all my sons: I see happiness in every one of them.
I see you grow older as the photos have faded.
Years of memories just lay there until this day.
Newer photos I keep in frames
Even the faded ones are on display.
Memories caught in a flash
I will always remember you, son.
Your beautiful smile placed in wooded frame hung up on the wall

Just Breathe

The pain will go away.
I keep telling myself so to say.
Every breath I take feels like an explosion inside.
These days, it's hard for me to breathe.
Just take a breath.
I still keep telling myself that when I close my eyes, I can still see your face.
A part of me died when you left my side.
Is this what I am going to feel for the rest of my life?

Just breathe
Just one breath hurts so much.
I pray that I can once again breathe.
I wish I knew what was going on in your mind at the end.
To my son who left too soon, I will try to breathe for you.

Overdose

As I lay here with pills in my hand,
I swallowed them down, hoping not to breathe again.
This pain I feel inside will not go away.
I'm trying to take my own life.
I thought that was the only way.
As I sat and thought, "What is this life?"
I thought about the pain that stuck like a knife.

My heart cannot bear it anymore.
My soul feels like it can't survive this world.
I realized now that I was telling myself a lie.
I grabbed my Bible and prayed to God.
With his help, he raised me above all.

There is a purpose in this life of mine.
Without God, I would not have made it out alive.
I felt his hands on mine.
I was reassured that I would breathe again.
Without God, I wouldn't have been able to live.
even with the pain that cuts so deeply.
I know God is here for me.

<u>Empty days lay ahead.</u>

Empty days lay ahead.
I find myself apathetic to
Days are longer;
The nights are colder;
It feels like the ground is quaking.
I look down at my knees, shaking
Weak from a son that was taken from me
It still seems so unreal that you're not here.
My mind and heart are so confused, but my soul breaks every day for
you.

A Life Unspoken

Quiet indeed.
With a good heart and soul, I wonder why bad things happen, even
when they are out of our control.
I've noticed that bad people are always smiling and laughing as I've sat
quietly through my life.
Good people always cry with their tears.
I ask God in my prayers, "What is happening here?"
My words became a book, needless to say.
Trying to be honest and go down the right road
Why is it that people want to judge?
Why do people play God off as a Christian?
I'm aware that the questions aren't any of the above.

with crooked smiles and wicked eyes Only a true Christian can see
their disguise.
You only have to do what God says.
A life less spoken for is better kept quiet. not even if a word is said.
God says the first will be the last, and the last will be the first.
Please God, I do not know how long my silence will be.
I do not know when it will end. My soul cannot take any more.
Give me the strength to heal from this pain.

a quieter, less lived life because God has those who believe.
"A life less lived" is what I am.
I know God is on my side.
There is no need to speak.
God will take my hand, and he will speak.

<u>God children</u>

Watching them grow up from birth to young adulthood
like children of your own
I love them both
Watching them take the first step or hearing them cry your name
Just being there for them is a blessing, to say the least.

Letting someone let you be a part of their child's life is a miracle.
"A second family" is what I say.
Help teach them the ways.
loving them each day.
Knowing you treat them the same way

My God's children are special in every way.
Strong, courageous, and brave
I am proud to be their godmother.
I will always remain to this day

Friends for life

Living in the country I've met a group of friends.
We made a promise that our friendship would never end.
Staying up late and sneaking into graveyards
Walking in the night under the moon's bright light

switching clothes, laughing at jokes about boys and how it would be
when we get old.
Being friends means staying by each other's sides.
We had a friendship that would last a lifetime.

Years go by, and the older we get, the more we have families of our
own.
Some of us grew apart, but we kept in touch.
Our group of friends still has our "circle" that we will always
remember, and we are never that far apart.

<u>Departure</u>

As I sit and stare at the mountains that stand still, I can't help but think
of life just rewinding through my mind.
a lot of heartache and a lot of pain. belief in prayers, but the feeling is
still there.
Maybe time will be on my side, but the loss of a son still struggles in
my mind.
I can only face reality, but my heart will not allow.
I gaze up at the sky and see white clouds.
All I hear is the sound of your laughter and the smile you put on my
face.
The joy you brought into my life

I wish I could just see your beautiful smile just once more.
You are no longer in this world.
You just disappeared.
I only wish I could have saved you the way you saved me.
My love for you son is deeper than you can see.
I can only pray that one day we will meet again.
Until I depart from this world, I will keep you safe in my heart.

<u>The river</u>

Sitting at a river is so peaceful and calm.
Hearing the sounds of nature like a song
clearing my mind from thoughts
Seeing the river flow smoothly as the water covers the rocks

watching the sunlight glistening off the river
I see the reflection of the light.
as it shines like glitter
Taking in deep breaths while I sit here on the banks
I place my hand in the water.
See crystal clear
The river is where my thoughts are clear.

Sunset to Sunrise

As I watch the sunrise rise for the day,
I see the grass as tall as the trees,
I feel the wind blow against my face.
I felt as if time stood still.
So many things wonder through my mind, but I feel blessed with what
God has given me.
I think of tragedies in the past.
Maybe it's part of God's plan.
Maybe I will never know or know what I know at last.

As I sit and watch the sunrise,
I see the sun glowing brightly.
I see skies of blue and clouds of white.
I feel like a part of me is missing.
I will never know how to get that back.

As I sit and watch the sunset,
I see the sky growing darker.
I feel the wind blowing harder.
I see the moon shining brightly like an angel's glow.
As I climb into bed, I say my prayers.
I pray and hope God watches over my children.
I hope that we will be safe for a long time.
When I go to sleep, I wake up to another day with a sunrise and a
sunset.
I know with God that my heart can rest.

Ryan

You take my hand.
You seem to understand
Days turn into weeks.
Weeks turn into months,
Months turn into years.
We have been together through the storm and countless tears.

Our journey together helps us grow as one.
Loving you fulfills my heart.
You loving me in return made me grow closer to you.
I know we will never part.
You hold me tight when I need comfort.
You wipe my tears and give me your shoulder.
You kiss my lips when I need to feel your love.
You hold my hand just because

You take my worries and put them on your shoulders, so I wouldn't
have to bear
I know you love me.
You are always there.
I am very grateful for having you in my life.
I couldn't ask for a better partner in this life.

Every step we take, we take together.
Much more memories we are going to make
I don't think I can live without you.
give or take;
You being by my side has been a blessing to me.

I hope we grow old.
Die together in this old world.
We have conquered so much.
I cherish you more than you know.
We take each other's hands and say we are one.
We still have a long road to travel until God calls us home.

I know we will continue to love each other.
All we have is us.
Our family, which we treasure, is what means most to us.
I will take your hand and help guide the way.
As long as you don't let go, I know we will be okay.

<u>**Becoming a mother**</u>

I heard the news today that I was going to become a mother.
Filled with excitement of what's to come
Bringing a new life into this world
Our adventures have just begun.
As the months went by, something terribly went wrong.
Several months delayed, you were barely breathing when you were born.
So many prayers were prayed that day for God to let you stay.
Months later, I was able to bring you home.
My firstborn son
I'm grateful God gave you to me.
Becoming your mother, I know, was meant to be

<u>Focus</u>

Trying to stay focused on what's at hand
My wonders are revealed in seconds, and it's hard to glance at
I try not to ignore the family around me.
I'm lost in my thoughts.
It's too hard to talk about what I feel inside.
I do not want to be a burden, but I cannot ignore what is inside.

My children are now adults.
Handsome and full of life
I have to still be here.
watch them live life;
I cannot abandon my other two sons.
My son, and a brother who will always live in our memory
Learning to live with this pain
I cannot be selfish, but I have to stay.

Watching my two other boys, I hope to gain peace and happiness once
again.
Learning how things are looking down the road
I realize they need me more than I thought.
more than I know.
Knowing I'm still needed on this earth for them relieves some of the
pain I feel within.

<u>Walk beside me, Lord.</u>

Walk beside me, Lord.
Please take my hand.
Ease this pain I feel within. Your guidance is needed.
Please walk me on the right path.
Without the Lord, I would have nothing.
Walk by my side.
Show me how to get through.
Take my hand and walk me through.
Show me there is life again.
Teach me how to smile again.
Learn to accept the things I cannot change.
Lord, walk by my side.
Take my hand and lead me.
Guide me
Take my hand.
Try to let me understand

Stripped

Piece of me stripped from the soul.
forcing yourself when I said no.
thinking everything will be okay.
Did you ever think how it would make me feel?
You dug a hole in my soul that is taking some time to heal.
crying over the events that occurred. Shame on you for what you did
and said.
That leaves me with the guilt; I am the one who has to pay. You are
less of a man today.
Being stripped,
By taking something from a woman, you made me feel sick inside.
I do not know how you live with your actions against me.
You have stripped a piece of me that I can never get back.
I thank God that I am a strong woman who can live life and get her life
back on track.

She falls in love for the first time

She falls in love for the first time.
She doesn't know what to expect.
Knowing each other for such a short time, she gives her whole heart to
him.
Feeling as if it were right, she stayed beside him.
Meanwhile, unexpected news traveled their way.
They were going to bring a baby into their lives with much love and
much surprise.
They both lit up as they stared into each other's eyes.
Months went by, and they were still side by side.
When the time came, she delivered a precious baby boy who
brightened up their lives.
On one knee, he asked her if he could be hers forever.
saying yes to walking down to the altar
As they said their vows in front of God, they knew they would be
together forever. As time went on, their family grew.
added two more sons to their family tree.
Less and less she saw of him, the more she saw.
Being unfaithful and untrue
breaking a promise to her, she took off her ring.
Being a husband and father seems hard to do, so she left him for good.
She was left alone with three children to oversee.
Her children were here. She raised them until they were grown.
As she worries about the past, she knows she's not alone.
Giving love to someone else she knew would be hard to do
Her children are who she gives her heart to.

Heaven Awaits

When our time here is done, we will grow our wings and fly.
We will see our loved ones that we miss dearly on the other side.
Love and faith can grow so far and wide.
bigger than the mountains and the big blue sky
We have a purpose here in life. We go through trials and tribulations.
A part of life
No matter what we go through, God will always be by our side.
We can pray for answers.
We can ask God, "Why?"
He will answer on his time.
We are shaped and molded in our special way.
God built us all different, but he shapes us every day.
Until our time is done on this earth, only our faith can carry us further.
Believe in him, and we will be okay.
Heaven awaits us.
such a beautiful place
No worries, no pain.
It all goes away.
Until then, Heaven awaits us until our time is up and we can fly and be
in God's grace.

Where and when

Where and when that day comes
Where I lie helpless in this life
I will take my last breath.
I know I will be in heaven when I see my son.
Angels will sing as the gates open wide.
I know I will no longer be in pain once my son is by my side.
as I gain my wings and we both fly

Still standing

Still standing on my own two feet
Barely, so to speak.
Trying to move on with my life
Easier said than done.
You're always on my mind.
Your memory will never be gone.
Your memory will always be alive.

Back to everyday life, never the same
I see people smile.
I wish I could wear one on my face.
I wish I could feel the same.

I am having trouble breathing as I stand with the thought of you.
I'd do anything just to have your life back.
Seeing you alive again is all I want.
If I could trade your life for mine
No questions asked,
I would take your place.

Frustration

Frustrated at all times.
My emotions keep replaying like a rhyme.
not been able to think right.
Need time to rest
Each day is the same old routine.
Need a break from the world?
I need my mind to rest. I feel like my body cannot take another step.
frustrated with the situation at hand.
Too much to bear
I feel as if I cannot stand
Breathing heavily and trying to stay calm is what I need.
frustrated with the way life is today.

Deep Sleep

I feel as though I have woken up from a deep sleep.
For months I have felt such weight on me.
This pain is weighing me down since you left and are not around.
No more I love you
No more seeing your face.
I think closure has put me in my place.

I woke up feeling better than I have before.
Maybe the message is clear from God.
He took a lot of pain away from me, so I do not feel as much anymore.
I cannot let go.
I am having a difficult time.
Maybe I'm waking up from this nightmare. God has finally stepped in

All I can see is his lovely shine.
Missing you terribly, deep inside
I give God my blessing that you were mine.
I will always be proud to call you my son.
Only God knows what is about to happen and what has already begun.

My Journey

As lay my head down to sleep
I hope to see you tonight in my dreams
Searching for answers on why you left
I long for closure from your death
A son I carried from body and in life
I wish I knew your pain would have stood beside you
I would have helped you fight

My mind turned into a spinning wheel
Always turning from day to night
Standing in crossroads is where I feel as if that's where I am at
Where to turn, Where to look
Walking away is not an option
I wish you gave me a sign
Now I'm the one that feels left behind

I ask myself, "can I figure out clues"?
With all the love you must not been aware
You were there sparkle that was always there
Now you're not gone;
I will continue on the road I am on
I promise you now my journey just now has begun

A mother's love

A mothers love is unconditional.
Our love was sent from above.
allowing us to have such a precious gift from God to hold and love.
Always hold them tight.
Kiss them goodnight.
Speaking of stories before night
A mother's love is seen in plain sight.

Always be by their side.
Teach them the ways of life.
Show them how to love and respect them.
Show them the love we feel inside and the love we see with our eyes.
Our children need not be blinded by
They need to know a mother's love.

A mother's love is powerful indeed.
We will take your hand.
We will lead.
We guide you to God and the right road you need to be on.
We will take the first step as we walk along.
A mother's love explains itself.
My children know they will always be in my heart.
As their mother, I will never let go of the love I had from the start.

<u>God will see you now</u>

As your spirit arose from your body, you traveled to the heavens above
to enjoy your new life
walking towards heaven, brighter than any other light
seeing God's face for the first time
it must have been an amazing sight
God will see you now, the time has arrived
God accepted you before you smiled

even though it caused tears to my eyes, he gave you wings, so you
know what It's like to fly again
opening the gates with his smile for you to take your place
God will see you now
you waited twenty-one years; no need to roam
God sees you now

A brother's pain

A brother's pain when I look into the eyes of my children
Feeling of emotions
Feeling afraid
Knowing there brother has completely went away
Keeping inside their thought to their self
I know the pain and hurt they feel inside.
I wish they wouldn't keep it in like a bottle inside

Never before had they ever had this experience.
I will lend them a shoulder for the tears.
My ears for listening
My arms are here to hold them.
My guidance for where it leads them
I love my children all the same.
We are all still in great pain.
losing a son, losing their brother
Our family will never be the same.
As hard as it may be,
We have picked ourselves up and continued with our lives.
We will never forget our memories.
We shared as a family.
I will be there for my children. I will be there every day.

<u>Worried</u>

Worried about bills and everyday life
Trying to make a change since you passed away
Keeping busy, exhausted of the mind
Physically worn out, but that does not change what I am doing for the
Lord right now.
My moments come and go.

I have no idea how many breakdowns I will experience for the rest of
my life.
Trying to help others regain their strength and hope
I pray to God that he gives me the courage to do so.
I feel as if I am a messenger of God; I am the voice he wants to hear.
Worried, but I know with God everything will be alright. this is my
start; the beginning is right here.

Friendship

Childhood friends who grew up by your side
Every day you are in each other's lives.
Ups and downs are normal, to say
It's when the friendship comes back and stays.

Years go by, and we have a family of our own.
Watching our children grow up
We live different lives of our own.
Life can be complicated.
Near and far
Our friendship that has lasted through good and bad
Our friendship,
a friendship like we never had

As we are growing up in age,
Our children are grown.
We're still able to speak.
Our friendship has been through a rough road.
As we live our lives wherever we are
I know friendship will still be here.
We are friends because that is what we are.

Gentle breezes, gentle wind

Gentle breezes, gentle wind
Please be gentle as you pass by me as I stand.
Not too rough on my skin, not too rough on my face.
As I feel you leave, leave me with my thoughts.
Let me take my memories; let me take them in like a warm embrace.
gentle breezes once again, let me be as I stand here with a clouded
mind as pass me on bye

When you left

When you left, a part of me died.
Now that you're gone, I have so much to say inside.
I will no longer be silent.
I will scream how I feel inside.
I hope everyone hears
My Journey, My Story
It is all right here.

Using the words that scream in my soul
I hope it helps others.
giving them messages that they are not alone.
Anyone who reads my stories, I reach out to you.
May God bless you in life.
Healing, I pray for you.

Struggling through this life is not an easy thing to say.
We all have tragedies of our own.
Some are harder to pass.
Some we live with for the rest of our lives.
No matter what happens,
No matter how we fall,
It is all about how we get up to stand tall.

As I look into the eyes of my youngest son

I realize how much my youngest son has grown.
Time has passed.
It seems too fast. As he grows into a young man, ready for his life to
begin, I am so proud of him, despite his inner pain and struggles.
He went and took in what we taught him. Now he's going on with life.

He's a gentle soul trying to make it in this world. It seemed not too
long ago that I was holding him in my arms. He's an adult who
embraces me with his arms.
With so much love that I have for my son, I wish him all the best in the
world for his adult life, which has now begun.

Cancer

Today I heard the news.
They told me cancer was my issue.
explains the pain I feel within
feeling afraid, but being brave for my children and family.

keeping it a secret to many
I do not want sympathy;
I want this cancer taken out of me.
I need to be here for many reasons.
God help me make it through twice having cancer.
I don't know what to think or what to do.

Setting a date for me to go
Removing the cancer inside my body where it grows
Taking out pieces of me
Trying to get this disease that could take me away
I pray to God they save me.

A woman;
A survivor;
I stand so strong and true.
I beat you the first the second times.
As a warrior, I refused to let my life end.
Keeping my head up high, I had to fight. I won the battle.
beat the enemy within me. I now live my life feeling that I can defeat
anything.

As he touches my body

As he touches my body with his hands, I feel a rush moving in.
With every kiss he sends to my lips, I feel myself crumble inside.
I realized I could not hide this love inside.

holding me as tight as he can.
Missing me for so long now I understand
whispers in my ear, saying he's never letting go. He wants to keep me
in his arms.
holds me tight for the rest of our lives.

Eyes look upon us

Eyes look upon us wherever we go
Other looking through you try to see our soul
No one knows the pain or hurt
Or the journey we go through life
Sympathy is not words I want to hear
I keep quiet in salience so no one can hear

As eyes look upon us sometimes with a stare
Life weighs on our shoulders
Sometimes we cannot bare
We do not know what lies ahead
Others look upon us as no one knows what goes through our head

When Eyes look upon us
No one needs to know why
We all have our struggles and pain in throughout our lives
Sometimes I keep my eyes closed
Just cause I need not to know
Everyone has their story
It is up to them if they want it told

Land

Skies are blue
Clouds are white
Air flows like day turns into night
As rain drops down so do our smiles
Let the sun come out and shine on our souls.
Let a little light on our path guide us to a land without any pain.
Only happiness to the ones that still stand on the Earth's land

<u>When I saw you last</u>

When I saw you last, you had a big smile on your face.
Embracing me with loving arms
with a surprise on your face

Having conversations through the hour
talking about life and what you wanted
Where to begin and finish at the end

When I saw you last, I saw a young man.
who grew up too fast but still likes to hold my hand
I told you I loved you, and you said the same.
I hope you remember those words will never go away.

Sweet blue sky

As night sets, my mind starts to rest.
I gaze up at the sweet blue sky above and tell you that you are still
loved.
I count the stars as I do my blessings.
I may not understand why you're gone, but when I look up to the sky,
I know that is where you belong.

Even though I'd rather have you here
I cannot go against God.
If I could hold you one more time
I would let you know everything was going to be fine.

As painful as it is to let you go
I will continue to embrace the memories of you that I will always
keep.
You will always be a part of me.
No matter where I go

I will always look up to the blue sky.
I will talk to you there.
When I lay down to sleep, I know where you will be.
Up in the sweet blue sky where you are flying free

My Guardian Angel

Wings of white
glowing so bright
Beautiful singing voice you sing from up above
We all miss you down here with unconditional love.

The gates of heaven are where you have flown.
Standing beside Jesus
Hearing his beautiful song
I believe you are my guardian angel.
Looking down from the sky
Oh, how I wish I could see your face one last time.

Yours are the eyes of heaven.
My guardian angel
One day I will fly beside you and God above. I will never stop loving
my guardian angel, who carries my heart with such unconditional love.

Laid to rest

My mind knows you're gone.
My heart will not accept the day you left. It tore me apart.
Now all I have are memories in my heart.
Putting you to rest

Hopefully you found peace. Now you're in heaven.
Your pain has ceased. Finding a way to keep your memory alive
My days here are a struggle, but I know I need to thrive. I try to fight
these tears that I cry. It will be a continuous battle for me inside.

Ashes are what remain.
I know that is not my son.
Deep down, I know your journey in heaven has begun. I am jealous of
the angels that have you, my son.
The rest of my days, I will make you proud.
We all miss you down here on earth. Let God take your hand and guide
you to the promise land.

Broken along myself

Me, myself, and I are the only ones that can pick up the pieces of me.
I am all I have.
Only one life do we live.
I can't live with miserable grief.
Although a huge part of my heart is missing,
Forever, it will be gone.

I gather myself to pick up the pieces of what is left behind.
I am trying to pick them up as I go.
It is so hard and difficult to pick up one piece at a time.
On the ground, looking at what used to be my whole heart, which is
now gone.
Broken along myself
alone, for I am not
I do not go through this by myself.

Although I am the only one who can fix what is broken inside
Everyone sees the pain, even on the outside.
Given more than I can bear
I look down and see pieces everywhere.
Broke I am for now.
I will try to glue the pieces of my broken heart together.
Till then, I'm broken along with myself, trying to figure this out
altogether.

I need to hear

I need to hear that everything is okay.
I need to hear what my mind needs to set clear.
Hearing the sounds of crowded words
My heart needs to be reassured.

In desperate times, I call out for help, screaming your name.
Measuring the weight I feel inside,
I can no longer carry
It makes me weak every time I try. I need someone to say everything
will be okay as I go through this tragedy in my life.

<u>Nightmare</u>

When I closed my eyes
A nightmare had occurred.
Waking up with my eyes barely open and feeling tears running down
my face
I realized the nightmare was real.
Losing you actually took place.

I try to wake myself up from this nightmare.
only to see your face in my dreams.
Feeling Numb to Say
The words I try to speak barely come out. Only ears of pain and
screams are let out.

Falling to my knees
with unbearable weakness
Your life flashed before my eyes.
Remembering the day of your birth
was the best day of my life. Please let me wake up from this nightmare
of mine.

Dreaming that you are beside me places a smile on my face. Until I
wake up, you are in a different place.
The only wish I have in my heart is for you to be here.
Unfortunately, this nightmare is never ending.
It will never disappear.

<u>Shadows</u>

Shadows of truth lurk in the dark.
Hidden secrets that tore your life apart
Try to seek the answers within you.
I do not know where to begin with what happened to you.

Shadows cast a double shadow on what I may see.
My eyes are trying to focus on what may be
I am seeking through the shadows, but it is too hard to see.
Only shadows stay in the dark, as the truth lies when your life fell
apart.

Take my hand.

When you take my hand
I began to understand
Your loving heart is true to love.
You show me a different world.
A world I never knew of

as you kiss my lips
I feel warmth from your body.
When you wrap your arms around me, I feel your heart beat.
beating with mine

As you spoke the words of never leaving my side,
I know we can travel any road in this life.
So many crossroads we have crossed, you and I.
All you did was take my hand and stand by my side.

Your loving me has been a blessing.
The way you hold me, I feel the emotions are true.
As you take my hand, I now know what love is.
I truly understand.

First Moment

From the moment I saw you, I felt a rush throughout my body.
The way you looked at me with those beautiful blue eyes
beautiful smile; felt my heart beat skip a mile

Speaking to me so gently and softly
All I could do was stand there and smile.
Seeing you for the first time, I became shy.
You never know what lies ahead for you and me.

Years go by, and you are still by my side.
All the blood, sweat, and tears helped us remain strong throughout
time. As we stand side by side.
I know we can take on any challenge that we face in life.

Numb

Numbness I feel throughout my body.
My head feels like it's going to explode.
My eyes are blurry.
For I cannot not see
The words that were just spoken to me struck like a knife.
My heart races as fast as it can beat.
Pain aches throughout my body as I fall to my knees.
As tears roll down my cheeks,
like the creek flows with water down the stream

I feel as if I am dying.
not able to speak
Just scream;
My arms reach out, trying to reach you.
I still cannot see.

Numbness I feel
Inside and out
Feeling like I am passing out
My body took a toll.
I still scream.
I still reach out
I am still trying to see
You are still out of my reach.

Tennessee

In the hills of Tennessee, where I was born and raised,
I can still smell the leaves that fall on the ground to this day. I miss the
lakes and rivers we used to swim in.
playing in the woods until it was dark, until mom called us home to go
back in

No shoes on my feet
Running barefooted in the yard where all the kids are
Playing Red Rover and swinging on vines that hang from the trees
Falling down and scraping our knees

Tennessee, my mountain home
Where my roots are: where I was a child until I was grown
Remembering the sky, the moon, and the sun
Tennessee will always be where my life began.

Young love

Young love is so beautiful and bright.
Seeing my son fall in love for the very first time
Such a handsome young man, as he wears a smile
With a caring heart, he shoulders her when they are around.

The twinkle in his eyes every time he sees her stand by his side
He embraces her with love.
He holds her tight.
She wraps her arms around him with a smile.

Young love I say once again:
Seeing happiness makes my heart smile within.
Such two beautiful souls who found each other in this world
No one can take their young love from each other.
They are each other's world.

Why?

Why is the question the question that keeps replaying in my mind
Why did you have to leave so fast?
Why did you think your life should be in the past?

My loving son, I miss you so
Shattered into pieces when you left this world
Having trouble letting you go, why, son?
You had an amazing life ahead of you. Why did you decide it would
have to end?

My mind is not functioning right.
I pray till I cry at night.
Wondering why it had to be you
Such a gentle soul. Why did you want to go?
My hand was always out for you to reach. Time stood still when you
decided to leave.

Why?
I may never know.
Unanswered questions
Life not being the same
Why? will always be in my mind
My loving son, you will always be with me.
No one should wonder why I carry this with me.

<u>Celebrate</u>

Celebrating my son's life
Only cry happy tears because you've flown up in the sky
Celebrating you who was in our lives, it is hard to hold the pain back.
We still cry.
Cherishing the time we had
Treasure the memories we have. Your life will not be forgotten.
The love we have for you will never die.
As we celebrate you down here on earth
Wishing you knew how much we love you still, we will all miss you as
the days go by. We celebrate you, son, as you fly up to the sky.

One day

One day, my life may feel the same.
Pretending you're off to visit family and friends
It helps the pain go away.
My mind knows you're gone.
My heart will not accept
One day I may feel a little depressed.
One day, I am up again.

Lying in bed, knowing you're gone
I am left on this earth without you beside me.
Pain never seems to ease up any
I have plenty of inside
I believe it will never be empty.

One day I am walking along
In my head, I hear your favorite songs.
I still hear voices. So crystal clear
I remember your favorite foods.
I ask myself, "What am I supposed to do without you here?"

I know all these tears I cry will continue to do so for the rest of my
life.
Maybe one day God will help ease this pain.
I pray that one day I will feel normal again.

Other side

Take me to the other side.
Where can I hold you and see your bright smile?
Let's walk along the roads of gold and talk for a while.

Missing you deeply inside
All I want is to take your hand.
Tell you it will be alright.
I wish I could visit heaven just for one day to say how much I love
you.
That will never die.

On the other side, we can sit on a bench.
Sitting next to each other and talking like when you were alive
You will always be my son.
Being your mother has been an honor.
Never will that change.
I wish I could visit you just for one day.
I want to hear the words from you that I will be okay.

Book of life

The book of life has many pages.
Many chapters
There are many meanings to one's life.
We are all in the book of life.
The beginning is where we all start.
The middle is when it counts.
Then ending holds importance.
We keep turning pages to continue to write our life story.
The Book of Life contains all of our names.
We all have a story that needs to be told.
Reading chapters as you flip through
Book of life
What is the story you hold?

Dream

In the state of mind
Dreams open a world we can only see when we sleep.
When our mind is at peace,

When the night falls, the moon rises.
As I drift into sleep, I pray I see you in my dreams.
Conversations between you and me

When day arrives, the sun rises.
Dreams disappear when our eyes are open.
Closing my eyes shut just to see you with me
Dreams I hold on to make me feel close to you.
When I dream, I do not want to wake up without you.

You are forever in my heart.
Dreams, I believe, are the only way I can be with you.
What I dream when I dream is a part of my heart. My heart is you.

Long road

A long road lies ahead.
The travel has already been exhausting.
No directions I have
Just a long journey ahead.
May I find what I am looking for?
Down this long road I travel on
I see darkness.
Trying to find the light
Bumps and holes in this winding road
I try to keep standing.
Trying not to give up
I still have a long way to go.
Down this long road I travel, I hope to find my way.
Wherever I get to where I am going, I pray I get there someday.

Grandmother's hand

Grandmother's hands are so fragile and old.
looking at her hands I know her story needs to be told.
As I think of my grandmother
I see the beauty she held.
Her eyes spoke truth.
Her voice always sang to God from above about how she loved Jesus
and his sweet love.

Her hands played music for us to hear.
If heaven had a choir, I felt like I was there.
Grandmother's hands, which she used often for prayer
She held her family tight.
in her heart
in her embrace
My grandmother's hands tell a unique story of a humble woman who
took her place in this world by God's grace.

When my grandmother entered a state of sickness
I spoke my last words to her.
I knew she was ready to gain her wings.
She was ready to fly and sing.
When I held my grandmother's hand for the last time
Little did she know she would always be on my mind.

A man's best friend

A man's best friend has four legs and four paws.
teaching him how to run and jump
Raising him since he was just a little pup

The bond between them is unconditional.
Being side by side playing when he is happy or sad
Neither one leaves the other's side.
The best friend my son ever had

Finding a way

Finding a way for the words to say wishing for you to stay.
Nothing in this world can convince me that you wanted to go away.
Words cannot describe how I feel.
believing in reality that it is not real.
Was the sun out that day?
Where are the clouds blocking the way?
Why did you leave?
Why did you not choose to stay?
Finding a way to cope with life
Leaving this world
Staying out of sight
There are a lot of ways it could have been
The only way out for you was for your life to end.
New challenges come my way.
Losing a part of me died that day. Never will you be forgotten, my son.
I only wish you had chosen to stay.
Your life had just begun.

<u>Running</u>

Running towards the truth
I will not stop until I get to you.
I will try to run as fast as I can.
Even as tired as I am

Slowing down to catch my breath
I tell myself to keep going.
No one can do this.
I need determination so I can do this.

Helping hands reach out to me
Searching for what needs to be known
I will keep running as long as I can.
For you, my son, please help me find the way to find out what needs to
be known.

Wake up

Wake up
Wait, am I in the same place?
Am I delusional?
I cannot feel you near.
Why does this agony still linger?

Is it morning?
Is it night?
What is my insight into life?
It doesn't feel right.
Awaken, I arouse from my bed. Arduous to clear my head. Trying to
find the courage to proceed ahead.
determined to find motivation
I need to wake up.
Is this all in my head?

waiting for a solution
Passionate to discover your absence in the world
Awoken by reality, I feel as though I cannot move forward.

Wake up
I hear the sound of your voice.
Soothing as the sound may be to my ears as the calm waves of the sea,
Incapable of bearing for me to wake up
All I yearn for is for you to be here with me.

Dry your tears, little one.

Dry your tears, little one.
Mama doesn't like to see you cry.
Let me wipe away your tears.
Let me make them dry.
Mama is here, and everything is alright.
Let me take your hand to show you everything will be okay.
Let me give you hugs to let you know I am not going away.

I will sit beside you till your tears go away.
Seeing my son's pain or sadness breaks my heart.
I will do anything to make them feel better, not tear them apart.
As little as they were, they would scrape their knees or bump their
heads.
Nevertheless, they always had Mama by their side.
My children mean everything to me, for they are my life.

Best friend

As I see the tears from my best friend's eyes, I see the biggest pain of
her life. I hear her voice, She's barely able to speak; all she does is cry
and weep.
She lost a child in her wound.
A miscarriage she went through
Miles away I could not be by her side.
only talking to her over the phone from a distance.
My best friend is the best.
We have been through a lot over the years. I have not seen her shed so
many tears.
One day, she will be able to heal.
a little at a time.
A part of her is missing.
She is learning how to deal with
As her best friend, I will always be here.

Spirit

Spirit awakens me from a dead sleep.
Hearing a gentle voice speaking to me
By saying my name as sweetly as I have ever heard it,
I realize God is talking to me.
He needs to be heard.

As the moon shines brightly through my bedroom window,
I lean over and see my Bible right next to me.
I could not speak.
I realized he was answering my prayers, and
I feel all the worries he took from me.
No burdens were on my shoulders.

I am thankful for that night. Sleep was not an option for me.
Excited from hearing the voice of Jesus, "taking all the weight from
me,"
His voice I can still hear.
A voice that will not be forgotten
The spirit of the Lord was lifted as he lifted all my troubles in the
world.

The light

The light is so far away.
Still in darkness until this day.
When will I reach where I need to be?
I need the light to see where I need to be.
The light shines so bright.
It will help guide me in the right direction.
Only if I had the light would it help me get through my days.
lighting a candle in memory of you
I see the flame glowing.
This light is for you.
You are out of the darkness.
Now you can see. I hope one day you will shine your light on me.

<u>As days go by</u>

I see the pain in my children's eyes. Part of them is missing.
They just keep everything inside.
Knowing that it hurts to speak the truth about the day you died

There is no one to blame.
just questions why
A mother, brothers, and all family aside
Pain struck us like a knife.

As these days go by, I know I will always wonder why.
I can ask questions all the time, but no answers will be given.
Only you know deep down inside.
Now your gone
I have to focus on this life. Other children need me by their side.
This pain we carry will be with us for the rest of our lives.

__Goodbye__

Alone with my thoughts
holding my pain in my hand
Beating slowly, it feels as if I am fading away.
Begging God to take it away

weight unbearable to feel
My soul feels weighed down.
Down to my knees on the ground, I heard the screams of my own
voice.

Drowning in my tears
My fears came true.
The day crumbled when you left.
You decided to fly.
Rewinding time in my mind
I was never given the chance to say goodbye.

Walking for change

\Wanting a change to roll on bye
Grab the opportunity. All you have to do is try.
Taking it one step at a time
All it takes is time.
Seems so far away, just reach up and try
Walking for change
A change in your life

One life to live
All we have is ourselves.
Strength must build within us.
Courage buried deep
We take all of our hurt and anger and thrive to get where we need to
be.

Walking for change
Step by step
The clock keeps ticking; we must go.
As long as we are breathing, anyone has the chance.
just reach up and grab it for a change in our lives.
Walking for a change
Walking to get a different direction for a better life

Beautiful Boy

A beautiful boy lies in my arms.
Every wink and every smile warmed my heart.
A newborn so precious and pure,
I believed in a miracle.
Now here you are.

Crawling along the floor, you would go
Soon after, you were walking, taking steps on the floor.
Growing up fast, time seems to soar.

You played in band and drama class, were very book smart, and made
good grades in school.
how proud I was to be your mother. I still love you to this day. You are
my beautiful boy.

Now you're grown up.
Making decisions on your own: I cannot be there to protect you while
you are on your own.
moving miles away to the place you wanted to be.
Never would I expect you to leave this world before me.

My beautiful boy, I say to you, "I am proud to be your mother."
I'm proud of you, my son, and I wish I was there to help you through.
Looking back, I believe God let me borrow you, my beautiful boy,
who was precious and true.

Dear God

Dear God,
Please hear my prayer.
I see what is not in front of me, but inside of me.
Release these emotions, for I cannot bear
All I do is sit and stare.
I'm not focused on the life in front of me because my heart is in despair.
Please God, I need you to hear my prayer.

Give me the strength to move on in this life. Give me the strength to be there for the ones I love.
Give me the strength to get up again.
I have fallen to my knees praying to you from up above. I'm still in this world for my children, and one angel is in your sweet love.
Free me from these tears I cry. Free me from this prison that I feel I am inside.
Dear God, I need you to be by my side.

As you hear my prayers, I will do for you as you ask of me; I will do what it takes.
Let me know what to do. I am at a loss.
I am confused. Please God, take this pain away. Please God, take my hand through this storm.
I feel as if I am drowning, and I just want to breathe again.
Please God, let me feel life again.

<u>Raven</u>

Raven flies high at night like a free spirit.
The shadow of the moon in the clouds as wings spread apart
makes me wish I was a raven for one day.
Spread my wings and fly no matter how far I feel the clouds on my
face.
Forget about life for a day.
When day turns into night, all I want to do is fly.
Forget about the problems I own. Just go wherever I want to and forget
the world. Float up high and see the earth below.
A raven represents loss and death.
I want to go wild and free
go where I want to be.
So I chose a raven for one day. I will go to heaven just to see your
sweet face.

Depressed by anger

Anger has depressed me in so many ways.
I keep asking myself why. Why did you go away?
Was it the people you were around that did not make you feel safe?
Was it the fact that you were in the wrong place?
I told you I could not protect you wherever you went.
I do not think I can forgive myself even this day.

Anger I have been raging so deeply inside.
I know if I were here, you would still be alive.
Caring for you since the day you were born
As a mother, I know I made mistakes, but your death has me torn.
Loving you, son, and your brothers, has made me complete.
Now there is a dent in my heart since the day you left me.

Reflection

I see a reflection of your life and wonder why you chose this path.
A paved road was laid ahead for you. Now all I see are reflections of
memories of you. Mirrors of your actions do not seem to be true.
Gentleness remained in your heart.
It seems to be incredulous.
This wasn't you, glowing on such a kind soul, that you were
wondering the thoughts and pain that gave you scars.
You did not reach out to me; I would have held you in my arms.
as my mind scrambles trying to figure everything out.
When I look in the mirror, I see a piece of me missing.
Treasuring what I hold tight
Reflections of your memories of you in my life

Dusted with confusion

Nature's angry blow has covered the mountains in dust.
I'm watching a dim light as night falls.
Intelligent: how we observe an experience of proper existence
We prosper as the variance of life continues to move forward.

Nevertheless, speaking the word of truth
Denial of a tragic event leaves me torn within
A beginning always has an end.
Nature's call: blowing ears for hearing
My eyes are dazed.
My tongue has become paralyzed and numb.

Sensible to mourning
maintained by grief
The prison of the inflammation of sadness
Each day acts like an eternity of suffering.
closing my eyes as I travel
Travel to the world where you exist.
My child, I stay in a state of confusion over why you left.

Engagement

As I watched my son get down on one knee, he asked his love, "Will
you marry me?"
She said yes without skipping a beat.
I can see the love in their eyes.
As they embrace each other for their journey to start for the rest of
their lives, it is a happy moment for me to say, "
My baby boy is grown up."
Ready to be a man and take on the world today.
With his love by his side,
I know they will live a happy life.
He gave her his heart as she gave him hers.
What a proud mother I am to accept her as one of ours.

Louisiana

Louisiana holds the secrets that lie.
The woods around you are as dark as night.
The swamp surrounded the land on which you stood to take your life.
I think about that day.
I cannot help but to cry.
The water runs deep.
As the secrets in your heart
The Louisiana sky saw you that night.
Was it happiness you longed for?
Your family, were you missing?
Was evil around you forcing you into something?
I will never know what was in your heart.
Louisiana skies
So gloomy and dark
As you were walking in the woods at night, the trees stood tall and
dark.
You took your last breath.
Louisiana skies, where you were laid to rest.

First and my last

Finally, my love seeking journey has come to an end.
The day I met you, our adventure began.
Nine years have gone by.
We have shared our secrets, our love, and the rest of our lives.
Our bond is unbreakable because of what we feel in our beating hearts
for one another.

Take our hands and clasp them tightly together.
No one can come between us.
not now or forever;
Strolling along with you in this life, our eyes have seen too much.
There is too much pain for our hearts to bear, but we are still holding
on.
Our hands represent our hearts as we hold on.

The storm

As the storm approaches, I expect
It feels like the waves of life have pulled me under. I feel like I am
drowning in the middle of the sea.
All I try to do is reach up and breathe.
The waves keep coming as hard as they can.
I pray to God that he takes my hand and saves me.
As the thunder rolls above me,
I can only imagine how it is going to be.
Life turns dark.
How is this going to end?
What is going to happen to me?
The storm has passed.
It destroyed my life.
How can I build what I feel inside?
losing what was precious to me, I pray that God pulls me out of the
sea.
Rescue me from this damage.
I do not know what to do. If your listening God, please pull me out of
this storm and guide me through

Words whisper in the wind

Words whisper in the wind
letting me know how you feel within
I know you loved me, son.
I love you more than life itself.
You're trapped in my heart as well as my mind.
As I hear whispers flowing through the wind
I feel your presence as you go back home.
just to say goodbye one last time.
Hearing your voice, I will never forget
As the winds get stronger, I have to convince myself that you are here
no longer. As I talk to you at night, I told you that I did not want you to
go. I just want you to know that I love you with all my heart and soul.

The heart of a touching hand

As your hand reaches out to me with so much love, you stood beside
me through this rough road called life.
drying my tears that fall from my eyes
I couldn't ask for a better partner by my side.

Your heart is big in so many ways.
All you can do is hold me through these days.
With the greater loss, we feel this pain.
The heart of a touching hand
Is what you showed
Reaching out to me
not letting me go

When you reached out your hand to me, I was not alone.
It's difficult to say that I feel like I'm not part of this world.
You try to help me live life and realize I have to move on.
The heart of a touching hand
You reached out to me, trying to get me to understand.
No matter what happens in life, I can always take your hand.

It matters to me

It matters to me to see you smile.
It matters to me when you frown. It matters to me when you cry as
your tears fall down.

It matters to me when you speak. It matters to me when you feel weak.
I will be beside you to help you stand.
Our love matters as I hold your hand.

It matters to me how strong you are. It matters to me when you go the
extra mile.
It matters that we were together, not apart.
You mean the world to me.
All that matters is you and me.

I hope a thousand words

Saying a thousand love-yous to the sky
Someday, I hope, hear my voice
Someday I hope you see my hands reach up high
I hope you know you may not be here, but the love I have for you is
still alive

I hope the sky stays blue
I hope the gates still shine for you
I hope your wings are beautiful as I can imagine
even more;
I know you were beautiful before
A thousand love-yous I hope, float up way up to heaven's gate
I hope you hear the sound of my voice
I hope it's not a too late
May your happiness is all you dreamt of even more than you can
imagine
I am not happy without you here, but I hope my thousands words of I
love you reach up to you in heaven

<u>Digging out of reality</u>

Descending movement, I am on the ground
watching, waiting what comes around
without warning it feels as if my lungs collapsed, struggling to breath.
I feel as if the life in me is being pulled right out of me
Reality emerging in my mind as I continue to lay on the ground
digging my fingers into the soil of the ground until they bleed
trying to dig myself out of reality

Deceived by my son's father

Why did you decide to treat me the way you did?
I guess a boy who never grew up
You're not the only one who lost a son.
How dare you and your other half pursue what you both did?
Taking ink and writing a false signature cannot change the fact that he
is my son.
cannot change the fact I am his mother.
I pray to God that you and her day will come.

Petty actions and selfish ways
The narcissist sets in blood and mind
Both of you should be ashamed.
Both of you should be the ones left behind.
The only way you two know how to operate

My son deserved better than you as a father.
a woman who tried to step in and wished he was my son's mother
God knows the pain I endured from the loss of my son.
How angry I am at both of you due to your actions
I wanted to take my fist to both of you, but God told me to hold on and
wait. On the day I come, I will take revenge; you have too much
painful weight. I know you cannot handle it. Let me take the hurt,
anger, and frustration. "For I am God, and I will not let them get
away."

Bottle

A bottle calls my name.
I drink a bottle to take away the pain.
My vision starts to get blurry as it eases the pain.
I keep on drinking, thinking I might see you again.
The bottle is half way through, but I still cannot see the bottom.
I must have forgotten.
Why have I accepted this poison?
Inside, I feel awful.
Is this what I need to do to get by?
Now the bottle is almost gone.
I now see the bottom.
I have blurry vision, for I see in double
Realizing maybe I should not have picked it up, I ask myself, "Is this
what I need to get by?"
An empty bottle sits on the side of the bed. I cannot lift my head
because I am unable to
The more I take in, the blurrier my vision gets.
I try to stand up, but I fall instead.
Drinking my loss away
I know this is not the way
How do I deal with you being gone?
I know taking this bottle is wrong.

I try to ease what's inside.
Deep down, I know I cannot hide.
Facing reality is hard for me to do. I will put this bottle down because
of you.
Knowing there are other solutions
I will just pray to God to get me through.

A friend's loss

A friend's loss is beautiful but true. Please hear her story.
I will tell it to you.
She had a boy she loved with all of her might. He loved her as well.
Loved her like day and night
Together their lives were growing closer to each other, that is, to love.
They met at a young age. What wonderful days!

Unfortunately, tragedy struck. Her world just fell and broke apart.
She will never see the wedding they planned. Be husband and wife till
the end.
True love is easy to see as the tears roll down her face.
sitting alone as they say goodbye. I watched her just sit and cry.
Not knowing each other then, her love for death brought us a
friendship that will never end.

As I got to know her, we went to his grave.
The wind started blowing as the fence gate swung.
letting her know, I could feel the presence of her love.
Messages started pouring out as I said what he was saying up above.
This story means a lot to me. The young love that was supposed to be
meant to
A friendship blossomed from this tragedy. She has become my best
friend.

As the years went by, she finally found a love that she couldn't deny.
Moving on with pain still inside-she now has a family of her own.
The happiness it shows
The moral of this story is that no matter who we lose, a loss of a love I
couldn't imagine
I've seen the look on her face.
Now I see her smiling, and I know it's true. Even if you lose love
Love will eventually find you.

Future

What lies in the future for me?
I hope for peace.
Losing a son was beyond words.
Pain that could never be measured
Without your child in this world,
they say, "Time will ease the pain."
It has been beyond difficult, and I'm longing to feel normal again. It
hasn't been that long since you passed away.
I wonder what the future may hold, but
I am scared to ask; I cannot handle it anymore.
praying to God every single day and every single night,
wondering how my future looks
Not least to say, "
A part of me died that day."
The past has been difficult.
The present feels miserable.
May the future be wonderful.
Give blessings to my family, and I know I will live with this pain
inside forever.
Please make the future easier.
My future will bring peace.
May God let me forgive others.
May God let me see the future he has in store for me.

Words whisper in the wind

Words whisper in the wind
letting me know how you feel within
I know you loved me, son.
I love you more than myself.
You're trapped in my heart as well as my mind.
As I hear whispers flowing through the wind
I feel your presence as you go back home.
just to say goodbye one last time.
Hearing your voice, I will never forget
As the winds get stronger, I have to convince myself that you are here
no longer. As I talk to you at night, I told you that I did not want you to
go. I just want you to know that I love you with all my soul.

Mother of an angel

Becoming a mother was everything I wanted it to be.
The day you arrived was the happiest day of my life.
So precious and small;
You were an amazing gift from God, the most greatest wonderful gift
of all
Throughout the years, I gave you all my love.
The love will continue to grow with you up above.
comforting me the best way you know how.
Being a mother, the best I can
I watched you grow up to be a fine young man.
I am the mother of an angel, and I am now coming to you.
You are safe in heaven.
I will continue to love and miss you.
Lord bless my son, who gained his wings way too soon.
There will never be another.
I will always be the mother of an angel.

Haunted

Haunted on this earth
Haunted inside
Haunted where ever I turn day or night
Life is not supposed to go this way.
I am haunted for the rest of my life.
It's Walking in an Abandoned Home
No one's there; you're all alone.
You're trapped inside, feeling that you're never going to get out.
Walk around scared
Nowhere to run, nowhere to hide
All you see is pitch black.
Feeling afraid of your fears as they unfold in front of your eyes
Being tormented inside
Haunted by the truth that I cannot deny
I lie to myself at times, wondering how you are.
All I have to do is look down and see the scars.
Walking in fear
Afraid to take another step
Feeling haunted since the day you left. Haunted by the truth. Haunted
by reality.
I never thought this would happen to me.
My worst fear has come true.
My child has gone before me.

Mask

Wearing a mask is exhausting. Fake a smile, and fake a laugh.
holding back the tears in my eyes
It's hard to breathe with this mask.
Wearing my mask keeps anyone from seeing what is really going on.
My brave face is on.
the courage to thrive another day.
I try to hold back the pain every single day
My mask I will continue to wear to this day
Inspired
My son is gone.
He is now an angel up in heaven. He has inspired me in so many
countless ways.
Your blessed heart couldn't take the pain.

When I wake up, I try to thrive for you, my son.
I know you want me to live my life and nothing more.
You made an imprint that will never go away.
inspiring me for what is yet to come

The ways you have inspired are through your kind and fragile heart.
You were caught running,
chasing your dreams.
Trying to make a start
You may not be here anymore.
You have inspired us all.
My son, you have inspired me.
many ways, and above all

Moments like these

In moments like this, there is a choice you have to make.
Time is moving while we're still standing.
Be happy or bitter for the rest of our lives.

Moments like these are unexpected turns of events in life.
No matter how tragic, you've got to stay around for a while.
We do not know our purpose in life.
We just go on God's good faith and prayer

Decide for yourself how to live.
Remember, you are very much loved within.
Moments like these help us discover who we are and what we can be.
Everyone has a purpose in life.
Struggle through the pain.
Your life is worth the wait

I see God saving me

I see trees hanging above the road I am on.
I see the mountains as they seem like they could reach to the heavens
of the earth.
I looked down, and I saw dirt.
a dirt road that stretches and winds
I see rocks laying as they look like they are sleeping.
The stars above all I pray to the heavens God hears my prayers.
I will fall down on my knees and say another prayer.

Ask and yell, and you shall receive, the Bible says.
God, all I want is for this weight to be taken off my shoulders.
I began to feel lighter than I did at the beginning.
weights lifted off within as time goes by
I look up at the sky.
I began to cry.

As I am still on my knees, I feel something drop upon me.
I feel the rain come down.
Is God crying too?
As I started to stand, I felt God picking me up with his amazing hands.
I began to walk along this road I have ahead.
praying every step of the way
leading me where I need to be
I thank you, Jesus, for saving me.

Wondering what if

Wondering what if things could be the same and you were still here
Would we leave off where we left off?
Would you fulfill your dreams about what you were determined to set
out to do?
So many questions fill my head.
Why did you feel that life was not good to you?

I know we left off not in a good place.
I wish you had not left.
I know you would still be alive.
You needed family by your side.

Wondering what might have been
You are living your life as we discussed it back then.
Wanting a career and family
You said you wanted children to make me feel old.
Wondering how you would be a father and husband
I wonder about a lot since you decided to go.

Wondering what would happen if you didn't go
You were loved in so many different ways.
Life without you here will not be the same.
Wondering why you left
Wondering how many "what ifs" I can ask myself

loss of a son

When I heard the news today, I cried my eyes out.
Knowing a child was growing inside
I was going to bring a child into my life. I was overwhelmed with joy.
I couldn't wait till the day you arrived.

As months went by, I felt you grow.
Feeling your feet kick,
feeling fluttering, feeling like butterflies in my stomach
The day you arrived, I wasn't ready just like you. I was scared because
you were early. It was a fight we fought together,
just me and you. The moment I held you,
so small in my hands, I started to tear up cause I had never seen a
small child that size in my life. I prayed for a miracle that day you
arrived.
praying to God to let me keep you,
praying to keep you alive.

As months went by, I started seeing a healthy baby boy.
So much love you brought me
Our family was complete.
I vowed then to protect you and love you until the day I die.
Years went by as I watched you grow up to be a fine young man.
Sweet as can be with a heart of gold
You truly did have a purely good soul.
Unfortunate, I guess the reasons didn't agree with life, and you are no
longer apart of this life.

Miles away you were from me
I couldn't protect you the way I promised.
When I heard the news that you had taken your own life,
My knees hit the floor. I was crying and screaming. I felt like I
couldn't go on anymore. A part of me died when you gained your
wings.
I wish I was with you to hear those beautiful angels sing.

I feel I failed as a mother. I broke a promise I couldn't keep.
A loss of a child I never knew happened to me

111

I pray for you, son.
I wish I knew how much pain you were in. Until then, I will wait. I know I will see you again.

Finding love again

Finding love again was unexpected.
Guarding my heart: I do not want to fall too hard and get a broken heart.
Nevertheless, the connection was real.
I still guard my heart. I am waiting for it to heal.

bandaging my wound, you have done
whispering in my ear, telling me you are not done.
Taking my hand like a man should
Making my dreams come true meant a lot to you.

We had our struggles, even when in doubt.
Staying together was the only way to save your life as you save mine.
Finding love again takes time and is hard to find.

Taking our love and keeping it tight
Wrapping your arms around me
Make sure I'm safe at night.
Through all the blood, sweat, and tears, we are still together after all these years.

A heart of a broken mind

A heart of a broken mind
what seems normal is not anymore
damage of pieces left behind, unbalanced of the mind
when your heart bleeds with the weight of hatred and anger what do
you do?

Faces looking the other way with guilt
not being able to look me in the eye
caring less about how they feel
blame? Shame?
Despising the truth for what that might be
lies circling my ears
lies punching me in the face
what did I do to deserve this?

When it comes to my life try filling my shoes if you can
My son's death took a toll with all other events topping as they occur
The truth, unfortunately is still in the air
I cannot reach that high I pray to God I can forgive so many inside

Holding on to you

Holding onto you is easy to do.
Your memory will always be alive.
I will tell you how I feel inside.
When I first held you the moment you were born, I made them give
you to me so I could hold you because you were new to this world.

As time went by, you were crawling on the floor.
Walking came next. I held onto you, helping you take steps.
Falling down Trying to walk on your own
Your lower lip curled up as I picked you up, holding onto you.

As you got older, you made sure you got to class on time. You made
friends that you wanted to play with. Some weren't so nice.
I remember you coming home with tears in your eyes. I held you and
told you everything was going to be alright. While looking through the
window, I see you playing in the yard with your brothers by your side.

Playing and laughing always brought me a smile.
Typical brotherly love
Understanding the bond they share, I watched you grow from a boy to
a man.
Such a proud mother I am.
Holding onto you was hard when you moved.
You tried to go off and make a life for yourself. I couldn't even hug
you because you were so far away.
I will keep the memories of you close.
Holding onto you is what a mother is supposed to do.
Holding onto you, I realized I couldn't do all your life

<u>Broken</u>

Broken inside as I stand here alive.
My soul belongs to God. How do I fix my broken side?
How do I put these pieces together that I cannot hide?
Broken by what I'm feeling
Broken is what I will remain while the pieces lay inside.

<u>Surviving</u>

Everyday life is about surviving.
Trying to shake life differently now.
Continuing on is hard to do without you. Our future plans are no more.
You decided to walk up and knock on heaven's door.

Surviving what lives in me
I can't decide which way to go. I take care of my other children who
are still with me.
Trying to do daily chores
Daily routines
It sounds easy to do, but it isn't for me.

I see your face when I go out. I see your favorite things.
It makes me cry out.
Surviving these days is all I need.
It is hard just to wake up and breathe.

<u>Cruel intentions</u>

My heart sank with more news today. So much anguish.
The pain gets worse.
It will not go away.
Being deceitful with cruel actions
What have they done to you, my son?

Finding ways to learn the truth
How the actions of others affect others
Cruel intentions are on my mind.
I was in your life until jealousy, among other things, arrived, knowing
you wouldn't just take your own life.
Nevertheless, I need to know the truth. Why do I have no answers?
I do not have a clue.

God sees all. He knows where the truth lies. I pray for a miracle for
closure in my life.
Our family and friends feel robbed without you by their sides.
You deserved so much more in life. In our eyes, you will always be
our young light

Sparkling cries

Sparkling tears fall from my eyes.
wrapping the pain as I try to seek
Pain glistens with every tear that rolls down my cheek.
In a daze, I continue to weep and bury my head in my hands.
I close my eyes as I gaze into the darkness, leaving me breathless.
These are reckless tears of mine, and I feel as if I cannot blink.
Swollen eyes show these sparkling cries.

Sparkling cries shine with torment.
From your being absent in this world, I can only ask, "How many tears
must I shed before I get careless in my own head?"
Distraught by tragedy
processing the pain,
gathering and collecting my thoughts.
Sparkling tears on my face
Only a few understand true pain.

Brave

Being brave is not what I am. Having to face the situation I am in, I
have no choice but to make a change.
If I could rewind time,
I would love for life to be the same.

The unfortunate events took place, my loving son, and you are in a
different place.
Wishing I could change the past and wondering if I did something
wrong
I tried to reach out to you, but I was too late. You had already gained
your wings.
Waiting at heaven's gate

Being brave, they say I am
The truth is, I'm not the same, having to take life as it goes.
I am not brave.
I am weak.
All I long for is for my son to be here with family and friends.
For his life, I wish it had not come to an end.
Words from beyond the grave
Woman speaking to me and telling me what you say
I needed to know what happened that day. Telling me to let go.
Telling me I need to live again
What you do not realize, son, is that nothing is ever going to be the
same.

Reaching out for someone to connect to you was one of the ways I
thought of
Hearing you love me more, we'd always say
Never once did I tell her what we used to say.

Words beyond the grave I hear whispers in my ears
telling me all is forgiven
Stop being hard on yourself. Please live again for me.
I am an angel now.
Words from the grave you spoke to me, letting me know you will
always be in my heart. Not needing a medium to tell me you love me, I

already knew. I needed to know what was weighing on you. I love you
more than you will ever know.
Let me hear the words from beyond the grave to help me find out
about your darkest hour.

Beauty out of ashes

A beautiful soul who came into this world;
I have a loving son because of God's good grace. A handsome son of
mine
changed my life of mine.

Sweet as honey
Gentle as a giant, so gentle and kind
Filled with a loving heart, never leaving anyone behind
"Beautiful son," I shall say.
You are gone too soon.
You took my whole heart with you. I'll stay behind.
My work here is not yet done.
All the weeping I have endured is sensitive to my emotions as they
pour.
With my sincere hope, you are at peace.
I may not have your ashes, but your beauty will always stay with me.

Discovering me

Trying to find myself once again
Life is knocking me down.
When is it going to end?
Discovering myself is what I need to do.
My life will never be the same.
I need to find a new way to be me.
Finding myself means believing in me.

Trying to have faith in what used to be
My love for God will always be
Strength needs to build within me.
Courage needs to fight—a fight that continues still in me.
discovering myself in a whole new way
Struggling to find a way

As life goes by, we get older.
Tragedies change us in this world.
No one can comprehend what one feels.
Finding a way to discover me
A new me that will be healed

Standing by me

Stand by me in my time of grief.
I need you by my side.
not behind me nor in front of me. I need your shoulder so I can cry.

Stand by me as long as you can.
I will never let go of your hand. I embrace you with all I have. Stand by me.
I know it is not easy.

amount of stress among us during this time, but we never left each other behind.
Let's not give up on each other. Stand by me with all you have.
We can grow stronger together with all we have.

Cold wind

Night has arrived.
A cold wind blows among the trees.
Rain drops as cold as ice
I stand here watching the dark.
Feeling the rain hit my skin
It feels comforting from what I feel within.

As the cold wind continues to blow, I look up. No moon, no glow.
The clouds are gloomy and gray.
All I hear is the cold wind whispering away.
As I stand here to listen to what the wind has to say

The night gets older as it starts to get colder.
The wind blows as the rain hits my face.
I close my eyes, trying to imagine time and place.
As the cold wind continues, I will stand here until I figure out what
happened to you on that day.

No way out.

There is no way out. I am trapped in this world.
Grieving and pain are all I feel.
Losing a part of me seems so surreal.
There are no grave markers where you lie; instead, you were turned
into ashes.
There is no tombstone that lies on the ground. There is nowhere for
you to be found.

I'm trying my best to make sure you rest. having peace within your
soul.
The only mark I have from you is my heart.
There is no way out. I am trapped in this world.
I am scarred by your leaving.
I only wish I knew
there was no way out for the questions in my head that need to come
from only you.

Lost loves

Lost loves can be found. Years apart
You come together as one, like a beating heart. connected to one
another. No matter where life takes them or where they go
Always have the most love they find within themselves.
So they live their lives apart.

They can't see it with their eyes.
Lost loves as they find their way
Finding love for each other among their days
knowing how they felt
Maybe one day, life will have funny choices.
Who knows if these long lost loves will ever find their way back?

<u>The rise of God's hands</u>

God raises his hands in the air.
My child, I have your hand. Do not worry, I will handle the rest. God,
I need to rest. I need a break from this emotional mess.

I will raise my hands in the air, reaching out my hand to you.
Take my burdens and lay them on your shoulders.
Losing my mind
I do not know which way to turn.
The only way I know is to turn to you. Take my hand.
Take everything away.
I will stand here with my hands in the air, praying for you.

Angel's choir

Angels rejoiced when you gained your wings.
Another angel in heaven, they gather around to sing, praising Jesus
with their songs.
As you enter Heaven, where you belong

A choir of angels sings beautiful
I can only imagine the sound.
having you sing with them in their glorious heavenly sound
You took your place among the angels' choir.
I imagine you dancing around.

Angel choir, you now sing
You are a part of heaven with your wings.
May you be at peace now with the Lord above.
Singing in the angels choir from up above

Young love

Young love is so beautiful and bright.
Seeing my son fall in love for the very first time
Such a handsome young man, as he wears a smile
With a caring heart, he shoulders her when they are around.

The twinkle in his eyes every time he sees her stand by his side
He embraces her with love.
He holds her tight.
She wraps her arms around him with a smile.

Young love I say once again:
Seeing happiness makes my heart smile within.
Such two beautiful souls who found each other in this world
No one can take their young love from each other.
They are each other's world.

The pain I've endured

The pain I've endured I cannot explain.
Not enough tears could measure up.
The storms of rain
Crippled by the thought you will never return
only concern is why you set your soul free.

So much pain to endure at a time.
Makes me weak in the knees. You forgot how to smile.
I'd walk a mile just to get to you, my son.
I'd walk to heaven and earth just for you to feel no pain.
Instead, you left
You were never seen alive again.

enduring pain I have received
Healing I wish to feel free.
Feeling chained up in a cage
I wish this pain I endure would go away.

Knock, knock

Knock, knock I hear the hollow wood inside of its empty shape
As I look around there is nowhere to escape
Clinging on the hollow walls of this place
Being trapped by emptiness
Am I slowly drifting away?

For I cannot stay here
I need a plan to get away
Four walls holding me within
I am stronger for what existence is keeping me locked in

I close my eyes wondering what if I don't wake up
Is this the last of me?
I slowly open my eyes and realize it was all a dream

<u>Coping</u>

Ways of coping when losing a child
There are no right or wrong ways to mourn.
No matter how torn we are inside,
When we lose a child, we lose a part of our soul.
A part of us that will never be whole

Facing the truth
Deny with our hearts
Our minds are so confused that we are falling apart.
When coping with our loss,
not easy to say.
We have to face our tragedy every single day.

I've learned it's okay to cry.
It's okay to break. Part of coping is letting our grief set in place.
One day, we will come to realize
There are many questions.
not enough answers to give us in our lives.

A child's death is a nightmare come true.
Anyone has experienced this loss.
I will tell you the truth.
Does it get easier as time goes by? The truth is, the pain will always be
inside.

My advice to you is to keep memories locked in your heart and play
them in your mind.
Never forget the ones that were left behind.
Our sons and daughters who were born out of love
We will cope with our sweet, gentle love.
One thing I am sure of during this time
It feels like I'm dying inside.
All I can do is try to keep my head held high.

My life

My life, I should say, has not been easy. I grew up in the mountains
and the valleys of East Tennessee.
As a child, I was never liked among my peers.
always coming home with tears

Moving around is the least of it. I moved up in the country, where I
soon realized that is where I wanted to be.
Starting a new chapter in my life
Finding friends
Some friends I have had for life

Becoming new to love
Feeling things for the first time
like never before
Finding a place where I finally fit in
Unfortunate events caused me to relocate once again.

now in adulthood. I have made some mistakes.
learned life lessons
I still keep it to this day.
Married and divorced for the second time
Trying not to repeat the same old rhyme

Raising my children in my life
Watching them grow up
Time has moved so fast.
My sons make me proud every single day.
Tragedy struck when one of my oldest was taken away.

I ask myself about life.
Why is it such a struggle?
I have been a victim of many battles that I seem to conquer.
Having pieces of me stolen and beaten
So I ask myself, "Is life worth living?"
Yes, I am still here for my children.

Thunder rolls

Thunder rolls through the sky.
loud as the pain I feel inside
Do angels cry when they say goodbye?
hearing thunder as loud as it goes, light striking the earth
Making an imprint next to a tree
The wind is letting the leaves go.
Thunder rolls as loud as my screams.
I beg God to give you back to me.

Hearing loud bangs as I try to pray
Trying to find a way
Thunder rolls as time passes by.
Please take this storm I feel inside.
Forgive me for what I have done.
Please God, don't take another son.

Thunder stops at midnight.
Trying to hear your voice God
Why did it have to be my son?
I ask you, Lord, "what do you want from me?" "What do you want me
to do?"
Just say the words, and I will answer you.

As the rain pours down, I feel like I'm in the tears of heaven.
God hears my prayers.
God takes my hand and tells me it's time to let go. Your son is in
heaven.

In the end,

In the end, did it matter?
Searching your mind, trying to find the answers
Figuring no way out-trapped inside your pain
In the end, only heartache was to blame. In the end, nothing mattered.

difficult time you were going through.
You kept silent.
No one has seen your pain.
In the end, you were the only one who suffered alone.
In the end, your life was young.

Heart of stone
Such a gentle soul
Amazing journey lied ahead.
Your life was indeed precious.
In the end, you mattered to me.

Reverse time

Reverse time I wish I could take the hands and rewind them to the day
your life you took. Reversing time is impossible to say.
Rewinding my wish every day

Time waits for no one.
The earth still spins.
The rain still falls.
The sun shines on cloudy days.
The moon shines bright at night on everything.

Reversing time, oh, how I wish I could see time stand still.
Taking back that night
A night that time will never heal

Black as midnight

As you were walking through the valley of death, I was there for your
first breath, yet not your last.
I imagine you walking in those woods.
black as midnight
What came across your mind to make it all end?
I broke down; I could not hold you in my arms again.

I would have held you until you let all your tears out. Remember, son,
I was always there to dry your tears.
I used to say that to you throughout your life.
Wiping the tears from your eyes, "It always hurts me to see you cry."

black as midnight on the tragic day.
whispering to God why it has to be this way.
Now I cannot dry your tears. I cannot wipe them away.
My mind tries not to think of you lying there that day. In those woods,
you stood as if secrets would never be revealed, black as midnight,
walking in the woods.
I do not have words to say about when you walked in the woods that
day.

<u>Waiting</u>

While waiting for that special one to walk back into my life,
I had a chance, but I made mistakes by not treating my love right.
Looking at the picture with someone new
Being that it's my fault that our love is gone,
I know I should have been true.

Years have gone by, and I still see the sparkle in those eyes.
I realized my love for you never died. Trying to replace the love I had
Only regrets and wrong decisions are where I am at. With all the
struggles my love has seen, I say a prayer to God.
I asked you to bring my love back to me.
As I told myself, I would never find another.
I will wait until the day my love returns to me.

Wars and battles

Wars and battles within my head
Fighting among my thoughts
like pulling the trigger on a gun
I maintain this war inside instead.
Imagine what could have been.
I barged with too many questions in my head.
Wars and battles within myself
I try to defeat
All I know is that I am worn down and beat.

Battles lay ahead of us on this road.
Wars are so difficult to focus
we think to ourselves what went wrong
A life so precious indeed
A mother's intuition I know you needed me.
I continue to fight with this war in my mind.
Helpless, I repeat to myself, "why you think your life was worth
leaving behind?"

<u>With you by my side</u>

With you by my side
I wouldn't ask for anyone else.
Hard times have come and gone.
all the ways you took my hand and led the way.

Introducing me to something new
I believe fate brought us together.
Fate had already known
As we grow in life, we will always have each other.

<u>Clock</u>

What is the time?
Numbers in the circle
As the hands move and tick
Watching the clock
Waiting for something to click
As time goes by
I sit and stare.
I do not know why.
Hopeful events will take place.
Maybe good news will come my way.

Tick tock goes the clock on the wall.
I glance and wonder what will happen, if anything at all. I hear the
sound when the clock strikes twelve.
I will sit here, posing like a figurine on a shelf.
Time will only tell.
Intense excitement for what will be revealed
Will time be on my side?
I wonder what will lay in my path as that clock strike is near.

<u>Silence</u>

As I lay here in silence, tears roll down my face
Never known of such pain
My mind often wanders why
Even though I will know the answer
All I know life will never be the same

Your face appears in my eyes most of the time
Hearing the sound of your voice to me is like soothing rhyme
The laughter you bring
To see a smile on your face
Nor will I ever forget the warmth of your sweet embrace
Such a young soul
Memories flash in my mind beyond my control
reality is so cruel
I will never see you again on this world
So I hold on tight with the love and memories in my heart
You will always be there
Your departure from me is too much to bare
All I ask of you, when I lay myself to rest, you wait for me there.

Daddy's voice

My phone rang, and it was my dad on the other end.
Accepting the call, I saw his face on the screen.
voice shaking with concern
Telling me that my son's life has come to an end
I paused because I couldn't understand him.
repeating what he said
I began to scream when I saw the look on his face and realized I had
no idea what had happened to my son.

I fell to my knees trying to reach for the door.
My love had to hold me down. I was trying to leave, but he wouldn't
let me go.
He held me in his arms while I was on the floor.
The next day, I received another call.
My dad was on the other end once again.
My daddy's voice
crying and saying he didn't want to be the one to tell me
He thought I knew

forgiveness he asked of me, but there was nothing to forgive.
He was there for me when I needed him the most.
We had never cried together before.
I'd only ever seen my father cry once before.
long time ago, when I was a child.
Our tears flowed together as my daddy's voice was shaky.
All I could tell him was that I loved him for being there.

As I look behind me

As I look behind me, I see clouds of gray staring back at me.
overcast, just the way my heart stays
I look back at these past few months, and I cannot help but notice all
the pain.
God took a lot off my shoulders. He decided to take some of the
weight off my shoulders.

Sympathy I do not wish to have
Hearing our story about how you lived your life
Suicide was not the answer, so to speak.
I know your state of mind. You were weak.
Too weak to fight your battle alone without speaking to anyone

You were not a burden. You were wrong.
So much love you brought to my life. Everyone who knew you loved
you beyond
The pain you were feeling I cannot measure the weight on your
shoulders.
not speaking for months before you left. I feel like I have failed you.
I couldn't do anything.

A few days before your new journey
I tried to contact you to tell you how much I loved you.
I never got to say goodbye.
Only if I were there, I would hold your hand so you would not cry.

You were found by strangers who wore the badge. I can't imagine the
thoughts they had.
collapsing to the floor when I heard you were gone.
Not my baby, not my son
Not knowing what happened except that you were not alive anymore
All the pain weighed me down to the floor.
Knowing I wasn't going to see my son anymore

<u>Secrets</u>

What secrets do you know?
How many do you hide?
How do you breathe when lies move with your breath?
guilty as sin when betrayed me when it came my son
Secrets lie deep and dark.
Living day by day, how can you even walk?
How do you keep your strength?
Believing evil lives inside you
Explains everything has caught up to date
Secrets are good.
Secrets are bad.
The truth always has a way of showing itself while the lies it contains
are hidden.
What secret are you hiding?
Is it too much to bare?
Only secrets obtain what I need to hear
What happened to my son while he was there?

Painful disguise

What did you wear on your face, my son?
What made you think you would be better off dead than alive?
Why did you try to put on another face to hide the pain inside?
Why did you speak the words "help me" when you were alive?

Were you not able to speak the words?
Were you too ashamed to share your pain?
Were you embarrassed?
Why did you not confine anyone?
Loved ones who you could talk to freely would have helped you
through, including me.
Why did you choose to keep your pain a secret and suffer silently?

I may know the answers to
I do know many questions have been left unanswered.
I was hoping you were all right.
Instead, I get the worst news of my life.

Hurtful words

Hurtful words that I hear from your lips
Staying around just to hurt me with another day
Using words as weapons to break me
You wouldn't let me go away.
Guessing your time, you just want to waste it away.

Married we were; together we are not.
You decided to try to take my life, so you thought
Being beaten and bruised
with every kick and punch
It hurt so much.
I started feeling numb.
Wrapping your hands around my throat
I couldn't breathe.
All of a sudden, you let go.

As I sat down, feeling roughed up
Tears came down my face.
I couldn't feel them.
I believe God was holding me and protecting me that night.
A night you tried to take my life

Nervous edge

Nerves on edge
feeling rattle in my veins
I'm breathing harder with each beat of my heart.
Emotions are flying high. My mind is going wild.
Feeling the edge of my nerves
When is it going to end?

Anxiety exploding as if it were the Fourth of July.
My words running into each other as they collide. Trying to calm
myself down.
Nerves on edge
What can I do?
There are no words how much weight I feel. The emotions inside, the
tears I cried
When will I be able to handle my nerves when I just heard that my son
died?

Swallow my pride, just stay away

Swallow my pride and let every terrible action done against me ride
Hand it to God; a huge fight is too much to handle when I've already
lost my son's life.
You, daring to be cruel to me for unknown reasons to many,
I am not afraid of the enemy.

I am real; I am not pretending to be someone or something I am not.
I regret that you are the father of my children at all hours of the day
and night.
I beg God to remove you from my sight and from my life.
My children who refuse to speak your name
Being said, your horrible actions towards my children drove them
away.

You blame me every chance you are given to cover up your actions.
I'm guessing you have someone to blame.
Your actions are considered not to be at fault.
You disguise your lies to appear to others as the truth, whether they
believe you or not.

My children became my life while you lived yours.
It is in your best interest to stay away.
I think to myself, "I know he would still be here if you had just stayed
away like all the years you were gone."
Now I suffer from the loss of my son.

Suicide

When someone decides to take their own life, they do not think of the
pain they leave behind.
leaving others in tears and disbelief
That someone is no longer here among us.
Pain is left in our hearts.
Their mind is not in the right state.
When someone suffers mentally with no help, it can be too late.

Others hide it well, while some show signs. Go get them help.
Reach out your hand and do what it takes to make them well.
I failed my son.
for he is no longer here. He decided to take his life in his younger
years.
I am clueless as to what I did not know.
I live with regret; how could I not know?

When someone decides not to live life anymore
Please do not give up on the ones we love.
Stand by their side.
Let us stand and fight for the ones who mean the most to us.
Give them hope, love, and a chance.
Assure them they are not alone.
Let them know someone is on their side.
Guide them to where they need to be.
When someone decides to take their life, there is no turning back for
what could have been.
Just hold them tight.
Smile and just take their hand.

Suicide Hot lines (International included)

#988
United States

Argentina: +5402234930430Australia: 131114
Austria: 017133374
Belgium: 106
Botswana: 3911270
Brazil: 212339191
Canada: 5147234000 (Montreal); 18662773553 (outside Montreal)
China: 85223820000
Croatia: 014833888
Denmark: +4570201201
Egypt: 7621602
Finland: 040-5032199
France: 0145394000
Germany: 08001810771
Holland: 09000767
India: 8888817666
Ireland: +4408457909090
Italy: 800860022
Japan: +810352869090
Mexico: 5255102550
New Zealand: 045861048
Norway: +4781533300
Philippines: 028969191
Poland: 5270000
Russia: 0078202577577
Spain: 914590050
South Africa: 0514445691
Sweden: 46317112400
Switzerland: 143
United Kingdom: 08457909090

Website:
bpf.org/resource/list-of-international-suicide-hotlines/

If you know anyone who is suffering from depression and thinking about suicide please reach out to The Suicide Hot line. Every life has a purpose. A life is worth saving.

**In Loving memory
of my son
Isaiah Nordgren
1/12/2001-5/25/2022**

Also,
Dedicated to my other son's,
Christian & Caleb Nordgren

sign my petition due to the situation at hand involving my son's
passing.
Go to:
Change.Org.
Demand Funeral Homes to check birth certificates for parental rights

Qẫ ç▩ ÇàÅởý M çẬÇà
Let's get this Isaiah Nordgren Law passed!

Written by:
Crystal Ellison

A Life Less Spoken is a collection of poems that express a wide range
of emotions. The author, Crystal Ellison, expresses herself in these
poems about the tragic loss of her son. As you continue to read, you
will be engaged in other emotions such as faith, love, hope, and
heartache as she reveals her life story and her journey. Her words'
passion for her feelings will keep readers engaged and truly open up a
world to everyone.

www.ingramcontent.com/pod-product-compliance
Lightning Source LLC
Chambersburg PA
CBHW051526120626
46551CB00012B/1100